LooK!

Liberation Unleashed

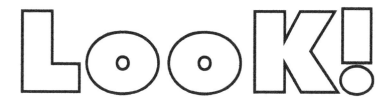

An illustrated guide to seeing what IS

Quotes and Cards by
Liberation Unleashed

Edited and Compiled by
Moonlight CR

Serenity
Publishers, LLC
ROCKVILLE, MARYLAND
2015

LIBERATION UNLEASHED

This book may not be copied or reprinted for commercial use or profit—No part of this book may be reprinted, reproduced, scanned, or distributed in any printed or electronic form without prior permission from the authors. The use of short quotations solely for personal use or group study is permitted.

First edition 2015

ISBN: 978-1-61242-868-0

Book design by **Arc Manor, LLC**

Published by **Serenity Publishe**rs, LLC

For more information, please write to:
chandi@arcmanor.com (about the book)
markedeternal@gmail.com (about Liberation Unleashed)

www.LiberationUnleashed.com

Dedication

This book is dedicated to all the people on the Liberation Unleashed forum—past and present, guides and seekers.

All quotations were taken from actual conversations that took place on the forum—this book could not have been possible without them.

Contents

Introduction
by Ilona Ciunaite and Elena Nezhinsky

Look!

What are you?
What is the self?
Is "I" a thinker or a thought?

If you find that your answers to these questions are vague, not clear, and you would like to explore what is true in experience, this illustrated guide is here to point you. This little book is an experience, a ride; it will take you on a journey of self exploration, where nothing is as it seems. This is an invitation to question beliefs and see through expectations, meet fear and look at simple ordinary life, noticing what is always here, now, in actual experience. This is an opportunity to discover what has never been lost and to look at "what is" with fresh eyes.

You are not what you think you are. We do not offer you a new identity, but invite you to question the idea that there is a separate entity behind the word "I", in charge of its own piece of life, managing and controlling what is happening, which has an identity—me. Belief in separateness is an organising principle, which is a foundation of how we see ourselves and the world around us. A shift in perception can happen that opens up a new way of seeing, relating, living everyday life and engaging in further exploration.

This book is a collaboration of many people from Liberation Unleashed. The quotes were selected from the forum conversations. A team of inspired people started putting those quotes on images, creating cards that were shared on Facebook. The best images with pointers are now this book.

There are several categories, one for each step of the journey. You can use the book in any way you like; there is no better way than your own. Writing down your own answers to questions is a good idea, if you like to focus more. Or just enjoy the pretty pictures and pass it on to a friend.

May readiness and curiosity be with you.

Ilona Ciunaite

This is a unique book
that will make you wonder
If all that about life and spiritual search
that you believed is actually true.

We start our search with some sort of un-satisfaction about life.
We feel, there is more then just what meets the eye.
We step on the Path, and here we are—
we become suddenly "spiritual"—special...

We meet with our friends and family
and secretly we feel we know more then them now,
just because they are talking about kids, and jobs, and weather tomorrow...
We keep thinking how boring all this is, and waiting to go home and hit the yoga mat or meditation cushion. We are doing inner work, we are deep...we are special...

With our spiritual search progresses we hear about oneness, non-separation, that we are one, and that we should love our neighbor,
and we ponder why we experience sometimes just the opposite, even though we put hundreds of hours into various spiritual practices
and have read countless spiritual books.

This questioning is precious and very potent.
We suddenly feel we don't know something, that something fundamental is missing...
This is a beginning. A beginning of questioning our assumptions about what we are
and what we are actually seeking all this time.

Even if we became more relaxed and less reactive, more kind and open, more compassionate and loving,
we still feel very much separate from others and everything, but now we know from the scriptures we were studying, that this is an illusion. We came a long way to this point where we are ready to set aside everything we know, everything we learned from our spiritual teachers and books, and look.

We are ready to look. Not to look and think, but just look.
Look at the reality as it is. Look as we never looked before. Look as we were just born.
Look with what is called "beginners mind". Look with wonder. Look with curiosity. Look with total honesty. Look without thinking. And if we are thinking while looking, look at that thinking then...

You are not alone in your questioning. Every seeker on the path comes to this point.
In a way, this is very unique that you are holding this book. In a near past to see beyond this point was possible only with a teacher who would help one with questioning main beliefs about "me", mine...

The art of questioning our beliefs called "inner inquiry".
It is very difficult to do this practice without proper guiding in pointing the mind to question everything what one wholeheartedly believes in, therefore the role of the teacher has been always essential. This book created to be your teacher, a guide.

Every poster in this book is a koan—a riddle that can not be solved without letting go of habitual thinking. Liberation Unleashed team invites you to your own inner inquiry and we wish you success in this undertaking.

Elena Nezhinsky

A Note from the Editor

I was a seeker, like so many others, of enlightenment, the ultimate goal. During the course of my frantic searching, I was fortunate enough to come across Ilona Ciunaite, one of the founders, along with Elena Nezhinsky, of Liberation Unleashed. Ilona encouraged me to stop struggling, and simply go through the process of looking at and questioning my most deeply rooted beliefs and assumptions with honesty and commitment.

And there it was, so simple, yet so elusive. Simple because there is no achieving, no drama, no struggle, and no 'specialness'—and that is also the reason for its elusiveness as it goes against all that we have been taught to believe our entire lives. In actuality, there is only honest looking which leads to a dismantling of all that we believed to be true. In the process, the imaginary self is seen though—that there is no 'you' separate from life. Life itself is all there is.

Liberation Unleashed helps people to see this, and those that do, in turn carry it forward by helping others to look.

The following quotations have all been taken from real conversations that we have had as guides with seekers. They have been chosen for their value as pointers, and we have put them together with complementary images to help others to look at what is real and what is not. Creating this book has been a way to show my love and appreciation to Liberation Unleashed.

13

As you read each card and its quotation, please, for a few minutes, forget all that you have read and learnt about awakening and enlightenment. Just let go, read and feel what each quotation is pointing to.

With love and gratitude,

Moonlight CR

The Designers

A few words from each of us who worked to create these cards:

Dirceu:

"Ready, vigilant and alive, you are there—at the Gate.

Then comes the guide who had crossed before. She takes your hand or slaps your face, depending on what you need, and guides you through the Gate.

You turn back, and see that there is no Gate, there is no crossing, there is no you.

And there never was.

ARE YOU READY?" (Elena Nezhinsky)

This teaser in Gateless Gatecrashers sparked up a fire inside me, after years and years of seeking in hundreds of places, and made me apply for a guide in Liberation Unleashed's site. Why not?

And I got a lovely and decisive guide.

After circles and circles—my mind always resisting what was just in front of my nose—she finally got me rendered.

For the first time I tasted the realization of a World where I was not. And it was very good.

It's true that mind goes on saying "I see" "I have" "I need"—but let it do its job.

Soon I was admitted to groups where people who have had a similar realization share their experiences, and some weeks later I read an invitation: "We need people who can produce posters to illustrate LU's quotes for Facebook".

That's not my job, but sometimes I made some graphics just for fun.

And that started a movement of hundreds of pictures popping up in front of my eyes every time I read a quote. It was amazing how the right picture just appeared from the photo sharing sites when my imagination tuned in to the meaning of each quote. Amazing how it was effortless and I could see how life just flows.

There was not a creator of the posters.

Thank you, Liberation Unleashed.

Dirceu Romani
Salvador, Brazil

··◆··

Bill:

I'm glad to be a part of helping get these cards out. What's unique is that each one is part of a real live dialogue from the Liberation Unleashed forum. If these hit home for you, and you'd like to know more, come and take a look at the site to see what its all about.

Bill Branczek
Oregon, USA

··◆··

Tina:

> Dear Seeker,
> just LOOK, really honestly LOOK.

> *Tina Huebner Patlyek*
> **USA/Germany**

··◆··

Ingrid:

> At Liberation Unleashed I finally learned to look for myself, instead of trying to get what others have said. I'll be forever grateful for that.

> *Ingrid Lill*
> **Germany/Denmark**

··◆··

Vince:

> Whether you are a seeker or not, what is contained here won't make sense. Sense is what keeps us insulated from what is real.

> Our language and the way our thinking has been conditioned has resulted in beliefs that much of what is conceptual is more than that. We have confused the map for the territory.

> If you are sufficiently courageous to examine your world view, then it is likely that some of the pointers contained here will do that.

> Here are a couple of Haiku (word pictures) one from before waking up and one after:

How easily i
tumble into the vortex
of thought. Just watch it!

The habit of me,
conditioned by life so far.
Now seen as a lie.

Vince Schubert
Australia

··◆··

Johanna:

I had had enough of gurus or so-called masters. Their words did not help, only created more confusion. The mind struggled so hard to figure it out even though it knew that seeing through this illusion was not some understanding that it could grasp, but a direct experience. If one had never known love, no amount of explanations would suffice to spark love into existence for him.

This is how I came accross Elizabeth: understanding, loving, simple and ... relentless (in this case she had to be). This process of looking felt like an abyss in which I was throwing away all beliefs and all stories I held so dear and identified as being a 'me'; a character assasination in a way. The thought of having no 'self' scared the crap out of me, but feeling trapped, there could be no other way but to 'look' through this one.

One night I lost all memories of the past and when a few hours later they came back, they were empty shells, no emotions were attached to them, they had lost all their meanings. When finally the illusion

18

was seen through, there stood the great freedom of having nothing to choose; in an instant 'me' had disolved into all.

My deepest love and gratitude to Elizabeth and everyone at Liberation Unleashed.

Xxx
Johanna Hebert
Quebec, Canada

·· ◆ ··

Lisa:

Take a look at these cards and the words near them. And then take a look at where they point. You can see this.

Want it, be on fire with it and follow the pointing arrows. Freedom is but a breath away.

Lisa Kahale
Hawaii/USA

·· ◆ ··

Angelika:

Completing LU quotes with images was an unforgettable experience. What I remember most was the kindness of the other team members who explained to me with the patience of a saint the technique of bringing the postcards into existence. Another memorable experience was the flow of creativity Dirceu and I shared for a while. Being part of the LU postcards team was a completely fulfilling task. May I thank all of you. :)

Anglika Graham Rau
Germany

·· ◆ ··

Ilona:

> It's been a great joy to be able to share this with many people and be part of liberation unleashed movement. I feel deeply touched every time I hear from someone that took a look and saw through illusion of self. LU keeps growing, with more and more people joining in, looking, guiding, sharing what happens further, passing the message on through various ways.
>
> This book is another gift from open hearts to brave and curious minds that are ready to inquire into the nature of what is. There is so much gratitude to everyone involved. With love,

Ilona Ciunaite
Lithuania/UK

··◆··

Chandi:

> Ready? Let's look.

Chandi Riaz
UK/Pakistan

··◆··

20

Look!

The whole thing is as simple as this:

There is no "I."

There is just what's going on, here and now.

There is just what's going on, here and now.

www.LiberationUnleashed.com

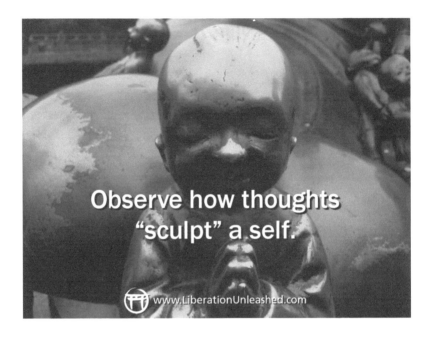

Observe how thoughts "sculpt" a self.

www.LiberationUnleashed.com

You will learn to observe how thoughts "sculpt" a self.

Watching this happen is a lot more fun than feeling "you" are "drowning in thoughts"!

For an illusory separate self, there is loneliness, loss and suffering, as well as neediness and striving. So all our lives, from early childhood, we may be searching for the oneness we lost by falling under the illusion of being separate.

We think that we are the thinker or the doer in our lives, not realizing that, like the rest of reality, we are simply life expressing itself. The mighty ego is not really in charge, or in control, or responsible for everything.

The sages and teachers point the way, but in our delusion we misunderstand.

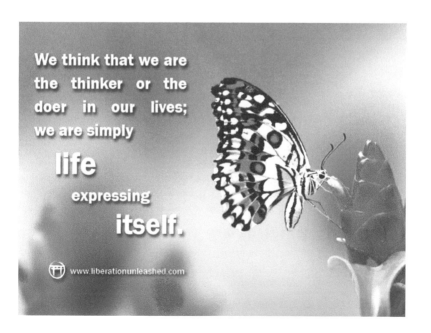

We think that we are the thinker or the doer in our lives; we are simply

life

expressing

itself.

www.liberationunleashed.com

Life, the only guru you need.
www.LiberationUnleashed.com

This is all about seeing the truth.

Now.

Look for truth every moment. Scrutinize everything. Instead of planning and "doing" life, there is letting life unfold.

Life invites you to a magnificent dance in every moment. It is awesome. The dance of doing the laundry, the dance of washing dirty feet, the dance of watching the news on television, all without resistance to what is.

Life itself is a beautiful dance partner and the only guru you need.

26

There is a sense of self.
It is not you.
It is a mind created illusion.

www.LiberationUnleashed.com

There is a sense of self, but that is all it is.

After awakening, that sense remains, but you ultimately see through it as an mind-created illusion.

It's not you.

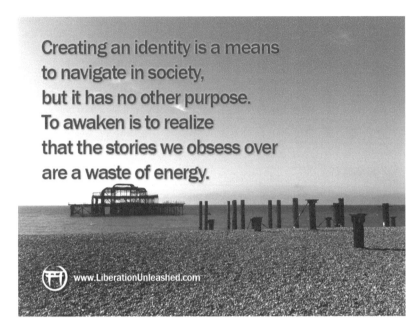

Creating an identity is a means
to navigate in society,
but it has no other purpose.
To awaken is to realize
that the stories we obsess over
are a waste of energy.

www.LiberationUnleashed.com

Creating an identity is a means to navigate in society, but it has no other purpose.

To awaken is to realize that the stories we obsess over are a waste of energy.

Please don't believe anything, but ruthlessly test it out for yourself.

This is not about replacing one set of beliefs with another one.

It is about checking out for yourself, in real life, what it is that actually exists.

Don't believe anything.

Check out for yourself, in real life, what it is that actually exists.

www.LiberationUnleashed.com

29

This isn't about making the sense of being alive stronger or more clearly experienced.

It's simply about seeing what is real.

It's simply about seeing
what is real.

www.LiberationUnleashed.com

Experience is happening.

To no one.

It just is.

The "self" is just an idea.

www.LiberationUnleashed.com

If you're interested, you can do this.

There is a way to look at "your self" from every angle until the inescapable conclusion is reached that the "self" is just an idea.

It isn't real and never was.

Once you see this, it's over for that belief. Then your human energy and body and brain aren't being consumed in the service of a lie.

Life feels better and easier. And if you have a sincere interest in this, you can do it.

Write down a list of everything you expect from this process.

How do you imagine awakening will make you feel, what will it be like, and what do you want it to be like?

That restless, compulsive searching for that one bit of knowledge—that one experience, that one insight that will make everything okay—is the condition a lot of seekers are in, and it can go on for decades, because there is literally nothing, no bit of knowledge, no specific experience nor insight, that will satisfy you.

Restless, compulsive searching is a condition a lot of seekers are in.

www.LiberationUnleashed.com

There is no "you." Dissatisfaction with what is, is the essence of the illusory self.

The self exists (in appearance) due to that very dissatisfaction.

This isn't about making the sense of being alive stronger or experienced more clearly.

It's simply about seeing what is real when you are not subject to the "I" illusion.

Awakening from the story of self does not mean that all of a sudden all of your problems are going to vanish—that there will suddenly be no more tough emotions or challenging situations.

This is not about getting away from difficulty, pain, and suffering. Not at all.

These are, and will remain, part of the drama of living a human life.

So please don't consider difficult feelings and overwhelming thoughts as a sign that you're never going to get this, or you're doing things wrong.

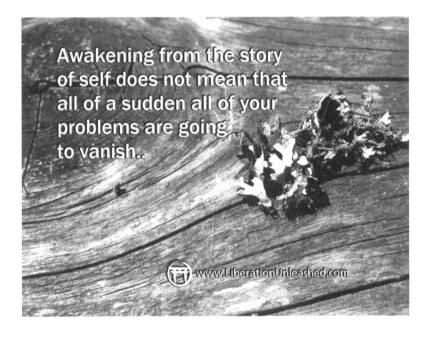

Awakening from the story of self does not mean that all of a sudden all of your problems are going to vanish..

www.LiberationUnleashed.com

"True nature" or "truth" is the simplest thing there is, but it gets lost under the piles of crap that get heaped upon it.

Then confusion happens. All you need to do is let stuff go.

Drop it. Clear the way.

Wipe the sleep from your eyes.

The wind blows, and thought processes happen You don't expect them to stop, do you?

www.LiberationUnleashed.com

The thought processes will keep happening for all eternity.

That is what's happening.

The wind blows, and thought processes happen.

Sometimes you are aware of them immediately, sometimes later.

You don't expect them to stop, do you?

Liberation is not a thought, feeling, or state.

It is really so ordinary that we have almost totally missed it.

It is through direct experience that it is seen. Look with fresh eyes at the truth of common everyday experience.

It's not hidden; it's just a shift in perspective.

Liberation is not a thought, feeling, or state.
It is through direct experience that it is seen.

www.LiberationUnleashed.com

Each person is different.

So don't expect fireworks, as they may not happen.

All of the emotions we have had in the past are still here; it just seems there is much less stickiness to them.

Look closely at the most precious beliefs that are close to the heart, those in the "no-touch" zone.

They are the ones that you really need to inspect up close.

You will recognize them by the feeling of resistance. Follow resistance.

It is here to let you know that another bit of the lie is sitting somewhere, waiting to be noticed.

Look closely at the most precious beliefs that are close to the heart.

www.LiberationUnleashed.com

This work does not aim to trigger certain types of altered states of consciousness.

These may happen (or not), yet they are entirely beside the point.

What is intended is to invite you to simply look directly at what is already the case right now, regardless of whatever state of consciousness may be happening.

Simply look directly at what is already the case right now

www.LiberationUnleashed.com

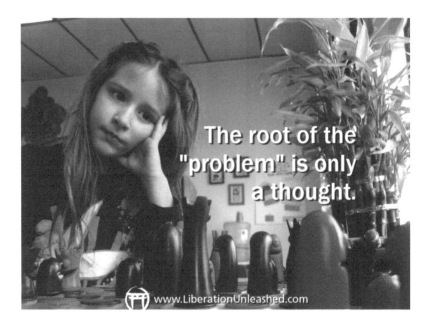

The root of the "problem" is only a thought.

www.LiberationUnleashed.com

Seeing no-self is like getting the diagnostic manual for suffering.

One has the means to get to the root of the "problem"—which is only a thought.

Outside of your perception, nothing changes with awakening.

The world is as wonderfully ordinary as it was beforehand.

You just become more aware of it, as you're no longer caught up in the stories you tell yourself about yourself. It's like experiencing life directly, rather than through a filter.

It's as if everything suddenly becomes very simple.

The world of words and concepts no longer clutters everything.

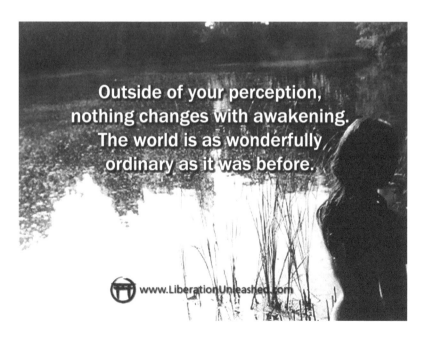

Outside of your perception,
nothing changes with awakening.
The world is as wonderfully
ordinary as it was before.

www.LiberationUnleashed.com

The aim of this inquiry is not to give security.

It is to see through illusion to reality. And in that process, we find that the person looking for security doesn't exist. Then the need for finding security and the need for answers falls away, too.

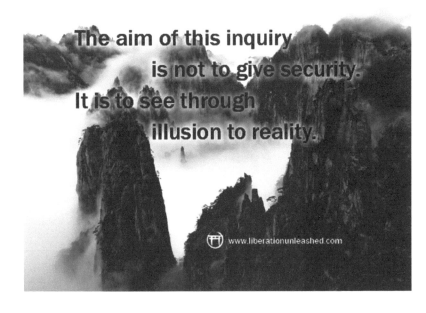

Let whatever comes, come.

Just look at it, even fear.

Notice that the fear is the result of what is being thought.

> # We are afraid
> # to lose our story
> # about ourselves.
>
> # Yet without it we see
> # what we really are.

 www.LiberationUnleashed.com

We are afraid to lose our story because it has become so familiar and dear to us.

What would we be without it?

It's worth taking the time to find out because what you keep looking for (so you can finally relax) is what you already are.

No accomplishment, external fame, material stuff, or appreciation will ever fulfill you.

The next time fear arises, welcome it.

Bring that fear closer for examination. Look at the mechanics of it. Observe and study how it works. What do you notice? Ask the fear to reveal its wisdom. Ask it what it is protecting.

Thank it for doing its job so perfectly.

When you become aware of anxiety about this process, the mind tends to distract itself away from the anxiety and the "hunting."

Look directly at the anxiety. Pinpoint its message.

Is it "If there is no self, I will disappear?" Or "Without a self, I will cease to exist?" Sometimes it's "Without a self, nothing will get done."

Check and find out what the anxiety is. Then ask, "Is it true?"

If there is no self,
I will disappear?

www.LiberationUnleashed.com

You will not disappear.
You cannot.
You never "were" in the first place!

www.LiberationUnleashed.com

You will not disappear.

You cannot.

You never "were" in the first place.

Existence exists and always has and always will.

What does not exist is this "you"—the imaginary ownership of a piece of existence.

Life is just "life-ing."

Anxiety may appear from time to time, but there is no one there to attach to it.

It is seen that "me" is just passing by—as a thought in the thought-sensation stream.

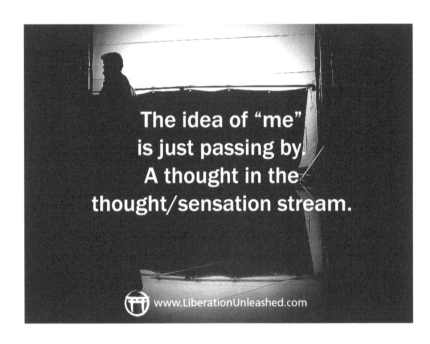

The idea of "me" is just passing by. A thought in the thought/sensation stream.

www.LiberationUnleashed.com

Is the fear of freedom bigger than the desire for freedom? Are you letting fear win this game?

Face it head on, without any reservations. Ask the fear what precisely is it protecting. See if there is anything that needs to be protected. What comes up here?

Bring that fear closer for examination. What is behind it?

Is the fear of freedom bigger than the desire for freedom?

Bring that fear closer.

What is behind it?

www.LiberationUnleashed.com

Do you ever experience a sense of terror when looking at reality too closely—as though you'll discover something you didn't want to know?

Do you ever experience a sense of terror when looking at reality too closely?

www.LiberationUnleashed.com

You're right!

This work is not easy.

But why live in denial, where all that straining causes you suffering that doesn't need to be there?

Doubt is to be expected. And it's not an enemy.

It only points to unresolved "stuff." Once seeing happens, the whole structure of belief starts to fall like dominoes.

Don't fear it; welcome it.

There is no one to control it. Just trust the process and let it be okay.

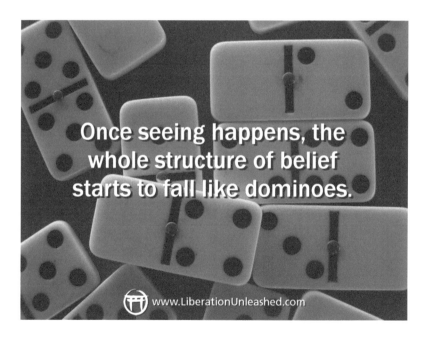

Once seeing happens, the whole structure of belief starts to fall like dominoes.

www.LiberationUnleashed.com

For some people, this process can be really intense.

Don't fight it, allow it. Go with it. Let it rip. Face it.

Ask the question, is it true that there is no separate self whatsoever in reality?

Let the doubt in.

Ask for the truth to be revealed.

For some people, this process can be really intense.

Go with it.

www.liberationunleashed.com

Close your eyes and search for the boundary of "you."

With your eyes closed, where do you end and where does the world begin? With your eyes closed, are you aware of a boundary between the skin and clothes, or is this only a kind of blurry sensation?

When you open your eyes, what happens? Is there a "you" looking out of two holes in your head? Are you doing the seeing? Or are the sights just here, without any boundary?

Close your eyes and search for the boundary of "you."

With your eyes closed, where do you end and where does the world begin?

www.LiberationUnleashed.com

What is being aware?

Is anything being aware?

Is anything doing the being aware?

Thinking is happening on its own.
Having control of thoughts
is just another illusion.

www.LiberationUnleashed.com

What is the "I", the "self"? Take a look and see if you can find a self. Is it "you" that is thinking?

Watch your thoughts, and see if you can find the thinker. Watch your actions, and look for the doer. You will start to realize that thinking is happening on its own, that having control of thoughts is another illusion. This large and complex program is running itself. There is no "I" making it happen. And if there is no self, there is also no other.

There is just life in another embodiment, the same life that is expressing itself through you.

How about the subtle witness?

Witnessing, focusing, intending, inspiring, observing, and watching are all processes that have no subject, no doer.

Every form of identification is assumed, mostly due to language.

Is it not possible that all this happens without an "I" attached?

It is a habit and language is like a rutted road.

It has an "I" buried so deeply in each narrative and story and general assumption that it is difficult to get the wheels out of the rut and drive on the road!

Here and now—

is there an inner and an outer in the experience?

Everything is happening by itself, including looking and seeing through illusion.

Notice this.

There is no effort, only thought about effort. Notice
that there's no one looking, but only looking and
seeing happening.

Everything is happening by itself,
including looking and seeing
through the illusion. Notice this.

www.LiberationUnleashed.com

Observe thoughts.

Just close your eyes for a moment and notice.

They come, one by one, a never-ending river of thoughts, labeling everything that is being felt, sensed, experienced.

Observe thoughts. They come, one by one, a never-ending river of thoughts, labeling everything.

www.LiberationUnleashed.com

What happens as you directly observe thoughts and actions is very simple.

Life carries on without thoughts about it. Movement occurs before its appropriation in thought—the "my-ification" of pretty much everything.

An "I" gets attached to everything in "my" world.

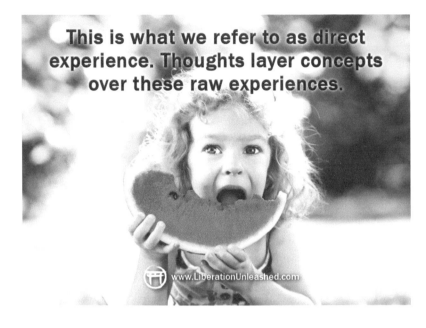

There are raw experiences: hearing, seeing, touching, smelling, and tasting.

There are sensations in the body (hunger, thirst, or pain).

This is what we refer to as direct experience. This is the level of experience of cats, dogs, birds, and newborn babies. Then there are thoughts. Thoughts layer concepts over these raw experiences. A thought or concept or label is never the actual. Some thoughts point to the actual, and some point to other thoughts. This is the realm of make-believe. This is the realm of "I." Is there an "I" in direct experience?

Sit with this possibility: there are lots of unexamined beliefs and concepts that are not necessary for life.

Keep looking into direct experience, and see how things just unfold, and how the mind operates as a translator of what is going on, as a concept-maker.

Sometimes this is useful, but sometimes it is just a distortion of reality.

The direct experience of music is so different from the mind coming in afterward and trying to describe it.

Music is hard to describe. When music is heard, no one hears it. It is an experience of hearing.

There is no gap: sound and hearing arise simultaneously. What was it that heard the music?

"Nothing heard the music" is the most accurate way to put it.

When music is heard, no one hears it.

www.LiberationUnleashed.com

If snow falls from the sky, what is doing the falling? Nothing is, the snow is just falling.

If wind blows through the trees, what is doing the blowing? Nothing is, the wind is just blowing.

If thoughts run through the mind, what is doing the running? Nothing is, the thoughts are just thinking.

If awareness is aware of a tree, what is being aware? Nothing is, awareness is just happening.

If life is being lived, what is doing the living? Nothing is, life is just living.

Thoughts are real.

The thinker is not real.

There are only thoughts passing by,
like clouds in the sky.

We say:
"I walk, I talk, I breathe, I type".
Is there an actual "I" that does these?
Or is it just a word,
acting as a subject for the sentence?
Change it to: "Walking, talking, breathing, typing".

Is there an "I" in any doing?

www.LiberationUnleashed.com

The mind labels everything that it focuses on. Look around the room slowly.

Notice how mind immediately starts telling stories and names things. When we acquire language, the mind learns to label actions: "I walk," "I talk," "I type," "I breathe," "I digest," "I sleep," etc. If you change these labels to: "walking," "talking," "typing," "breathing," what happens?

Is there an actual "I" that does the actions, or is it just a word that is serving as subject in the label?

Is there a subject in doing? While watching breathing, is there an "I" that breathes? Is there an "I" that wakes up in the morning? Is there an "I" that goes to sleep?

Is there an "I" in any doing?

The mind is a labeling machine.

Observe how it works.

See how everything runs on automatic.

www.LiberationUnleashed.com

Continue to view the mind as a labeling machine.

Its purpose is to name what the senses perceive, to label feelings, and to narrate the story.

Sit for a couple of minutes with your eyes closed and notice what the mind does. Don't pay much attention to content, but observe how the labeling mechanism works.

A sound is heard and thoughts describe what happened. A tingling sensation comes and thoughts label it.

Just pay attention to how something is experienced and then labeled immediately afterward.

See how everything runs on automatic.

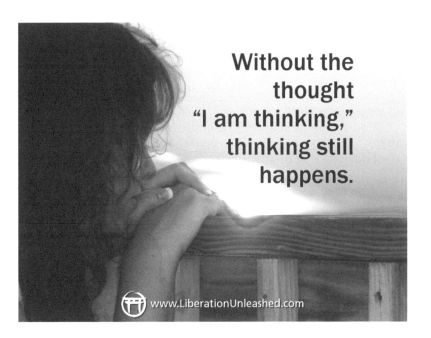

Without the thought "I am thinking," thinking still happens.

www.LiberationUnleashed.com

Without the thought "I am breathing," breathing still happens.

Without the thought "I am thinking," thinking still happens.

This extra level of "I" thought is redundant and unnecessary. It's like an obsessive tic that continues to poke up out of habit and conditioning, feeding on itself.

It's clear to the rational mind that there is no "I," but the defenses are strong.

A sound is heard, and thoughts about it arise.

The eyes rest on an object, and the object gets labeled.

Watch this.

Wherever you are, focus on what is going on around you, and notice how the mind names everything and tells stories about it.

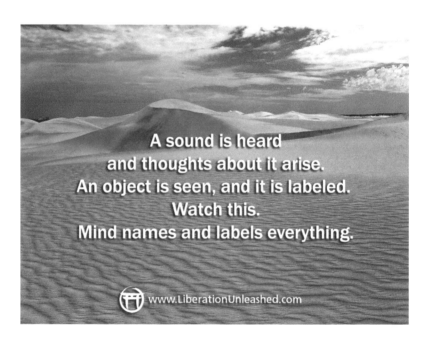

A sound is heard
and thoughts about it arise.
An object is seen, and it is labeled.
Watch this.
Mind names and labels everything.

www.LiberationUnleashed.com

Thoughts layer concepts over the direct experiences.

A thought (concept or label) is never the actual.

Some thoughts point to the actual, and some point to other thoughts, but the content of every single thought is just a story.

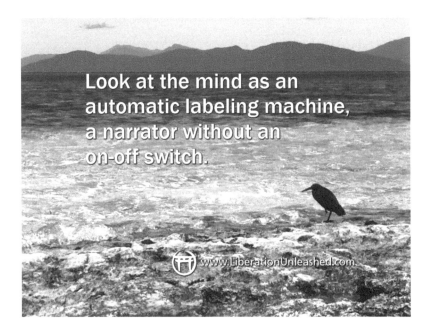

Look at the mind as an automatic labeling machine, a narrator without an on-off switch.

www.LiberationUnleashed.com

Look at the mind as an automatic labeling machine, a narrator without an on-off switch.

Look around you now.

Notice how thoughts spring up and label objects, tell a story about things, how they got there, without your having any control over them.

Thoughts are just that—labels that point to things, senses or ideas.

Is there a "you" that can get lost in thoughts, or is it just the thoughts, labels which are there, until they disappear again?

Thoughts will keep coming. But their content doesn't have to be believed.

Instead of engaging with the content of the thought, watch how it tries to suggest the existence of a vulnerable "I."

Thoughts will keep coming.

Their content doesn't have to be believed.

www.LiberationUnleashed.com

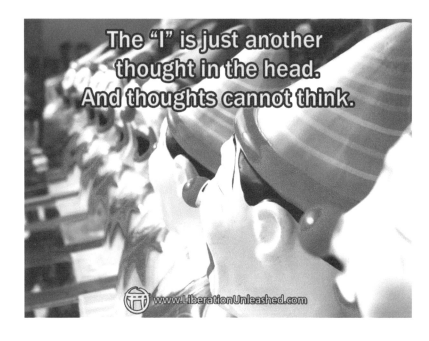

The "I" is just another thought in the head. And thoughts cannot think.

www.LiberationUnleashed.com

The "I" is not only an imposter, it is also just another thought in the head, the same as any other thought. And thoughts themselves cannot think.

There is no "I" that can be found outside of thoughts. Not now, not yesterday, not tomorrow.

The reason? It's not really there!

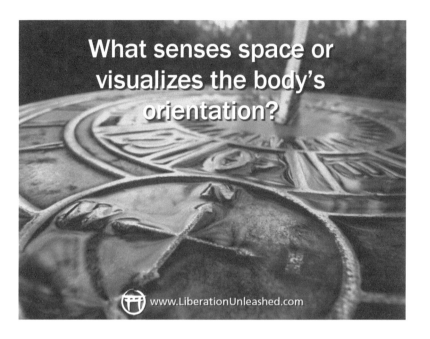

What senses space or visualizes the body's orientation?

www.LiberationUnleashed.com

Identification with the body and senses is one of the most common confusions.

What experiences a toothache?

What senses space or visualizes the body's orientation? What is the thing that knows the body is experiencing these things? How does it know this is "my" body?

"I," "my," and "mine" are simply concepts (labels) that don't have an actual existence in our direct experience.

These concepts are useful in a social context, but understanding that they are simply concepts is very important, because if you believe in them, they distort the way you perceive reality.

Notice how labels for objects are nouns and labels for actions include an action and a doer: "I type," "You read," "I smile," "You think," "I walk," "You talk," "We sit," and so on.

Examine the labels for actions.

See if there is really an "I" that does the breathing, walking, and thinking.

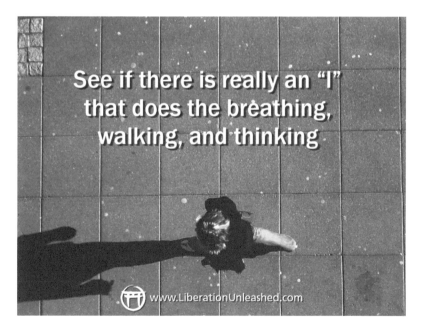

See if there is really an "I" that does the breathing, walking, and thinking

www.LiberationUnleashed.com

There is no self here except as a label.

You might imagine a witness, but what indication is there that this witness exists, except that witnessing exists?

This is an assumption we never even think to question, an assumption that we all completely take for granted: that for observing to exist requires an observer.

Your self doesn't exist except as a thought that refers to nothing.

www.LiberationUnleashed.com

Life isn't personal. Your life isn't personal. You and your experience are one, not two. There is no "you" living a life.

There is life as you experience it, and that is you. It happens with and without the thoughts of "me," "myself," and "I." Life is intimate but not personal.

You have no need to protect and defend yourself, not because everything's going to be alright and the universe is friendly (although that may also be the case), but because there is no "you" who can do anything. Your self doesn't exist except as a thought that refers to nothing.

Thoughts do not
mean anything.

www.LiberationUnleashed.com

Thoughts about yourself may arise, but this can be seen to be just another thought—a thought about a thought.

So what?

Another thought comes, and another.

So what?

Thoughts do not mean anything. If a thought is thought to mean something, another thought has just arisen.

Do you think there is a sufferer from which thoughts appear?

Isn't that just another thought?

"There is a sufferer here."

"There is no sufferer here."

Both are equally just thoughts, a story about suffering.

There is
something
happening.
This is it.
All the rest
is story.

www.LiberationUnleashed.com

THERE IS SOMETHING HAPPENING.

Please re-read this a hundred thousand times.

This is it.

There is something happening.

All the rest is story.

What are stories made of?

Look more closely at this question.

If someone just met you on the street, could they know any of your story except the part where you were meeting on the street?

They could see your body, but not your story.

What tools would you use to convey to them the supposed reality of a self, with a past, a present, and a future?

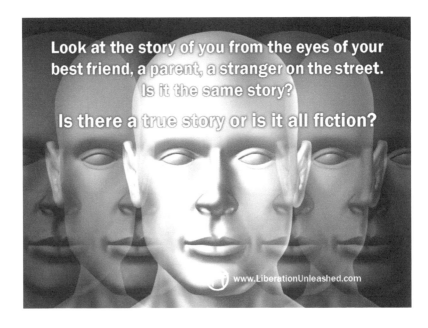

Look at the story of you from the eyes of your best friend, a parent, a colleague, a stranger on the street.

Is it the same story?

How does it change depending on a point of view?

How does it change depending on your mood?

Is there a true story or is it all fiction?

As babies we are not separate from our world. There is no place where baby begins or ends.

Then the story of a separate self is begun by our parents and family who tell us who "we" are.

By around three years old, the story of separation is complete, and we add our own bits to it as we grow up.

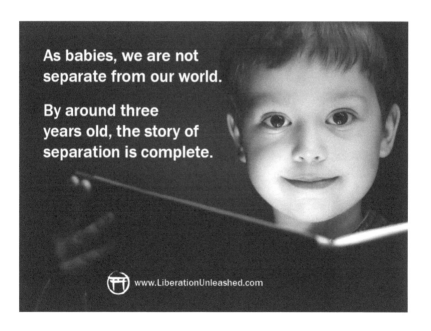

As babies, we are not separate from our world.

By around three years old, the story of separation is complete.

www.LiberationUnleashed.com

Thoughts build a small me, a grandiose me, a miserable me, an awakened me.

The variations are endless.

And it doesn't stop.

Just as optical illusions keep working, the imaginary self keeps getting built. But that doesn't make it a "true self."

Thoughts build a small me, a grandiose me, a miserable me, an awakened me.

www.LiberationUnleashed.com

Soon after birth, you were given a name and a bunch of data to help identify you: length; weight; eye color; date and time of birth; parents' names; and so on. You were now a little person who had a whole bunch of words and pictures associated with you.

Over time, many adjectives and qualities were stuck to you, in the same way you might put a sticky note on a white board. These were invisible sticky labels, though. They lived inside and were fed by belief, attention, and the meaning given to them. We are told we are good, kind, talented. Or that we are bad, lazy, worthless. We also learn to connect our value to the job we have and how much money we earn.

These are all words and ideas about who we think we are.

We are told we are good, kind, talented. Or that we are bad, lazy, worthless.

www.LiberationUnleashed.com

Can you see that "I am a good person," "I am a bad person," "I am attractive," and "I am ugly" are all just thoughts that arise?

That "positive" thoughts are thoughts that complement the "I" and that "negative" thoughts are thoughts that disparage the "I"?

Now can you look at what these thoughts are pointing to?

There are thoughts of "I am a good person."

What is the "I" that is the good person? What is the "I" that is the bad person?

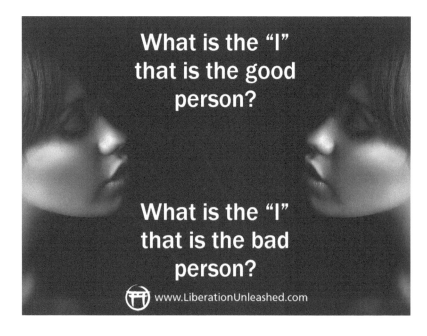

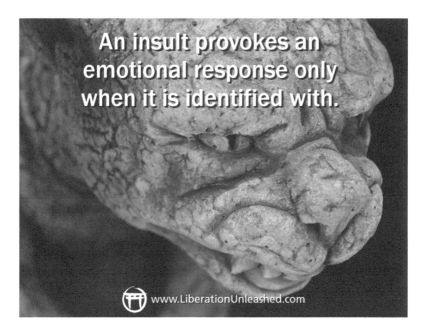

An insult provokes an emotional response only when it is identified with.

www.LiberationUnleashed.com

An insult provokes an emotional response only when it is identified with.

If someone were to call you "too blurry," there would be no suffering in that because no part of the mind would believe that.

If, however, you were called "too fat," it's much more likely that that might be believed and identified with.

If someone were to insult your family or even country, that would also provoke an emotional response because of identification with them. Flattery, of course, is the same in the opposite direction.

There is a movement to create a better, nicer, more lovable self, who will attract good things, be important, right, and beautiful.

www.LiberationUnleashed.com

Self-evaluation boils down to there being something "wrong" with you.

You believe you suffer from a character defect.

Then there is a movement to create a better, nicer, more lovable self, who will attract good things, be important, right, and beautiful.

And as long as there is a "you" with all these labels and features, then there is also the "other" with its own labels, who can threaten and harm you.

Living in a world of separation perpetuates conflict, violence, and the painful story of loneliness.

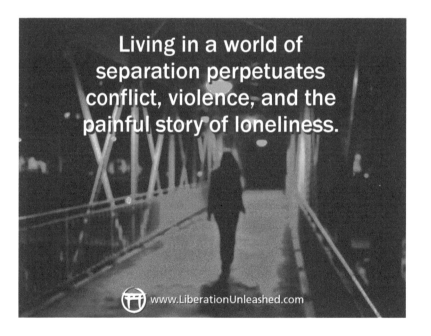

Living in a world of separation perpetuates conflict, violence, and the painful story of loneliness.

www.LiberationUnleashed.com

"You" don't exist. The "you" that you think you are is just that—thinking, thoughts.

Not real. Not in control.

Does a "you" do the breathing, or the thinking?

Is a "you" really in control of anything? Examine thoughts and actions.

What is really here? What is real? There is an experience of aliveness, but does that need to be labeled "me"? This identification with all these thoughts feels normal and familiar, but it is ultimately not real and is the cause of suffering.

And it is so simple that it is overlooked.

"You" don't exist.
The "you" that you think you are is just that - thinking, thoughts.

www.LiberationUnleashed.com

Is there a
hearer of
sounds,
separate from
hearing and
the heard?

www.LiberationUnleashed.com

Is there a gap between the perceiver of thoughts—
thoughts and thinking—or is there just one process
that we call thinking?

Test it with a sound. Stop everything for two minutes and listen intently to all sounds that are present.

Is there a hearer of sounds, separate from hearing
and the heard?

Where does hearing happen? Listen to distant
sounds. Where is the hearer then? With closed eyes,
check if there is a line between here and there.

Can it be defined?

Notice the sounds you're hearing, like the chirping of the birds.

Notice the habitual thought "I hear that."

Now just pay attention to how sound happens.

Take your time with it.

Are you doing the hearing, or is it just happening?

Close your eyes and imagine you are holding a watermelon. Imagine its weight and shape. Now open your eyes. What happened to the melon?

www.LiberationUnleashed.com

Do this little exercise.

Close your eyes and imagine you are holding a watermelon in your hands.

Imagine it so vividly that you can feel its weight, the shape and texture of the skin. Hold it there, sensing it, and open your eyes.

What happened to the melon? How about the sensation that was so believable?

That which is real can be sensed in one or more ways.

That which is imagined exists only in the mind.

Let's look at the body and see if there is an owner or entity controlling it.

Lift one of your hands. Either one. Move it to the right. Now move it left.

Look with your eyes at what is happening. Did a "self" move the hand? Or did the hand just move?

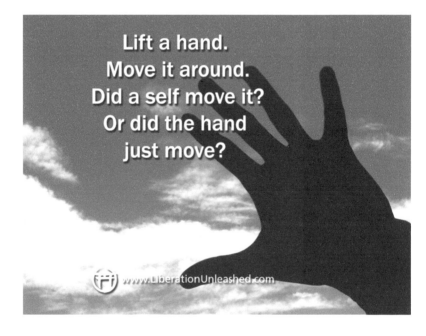

Can you see an absence of something?

Can you see an absence of something?

All you see is what is there, not what isn't.

www.LiberationUnleashed.com

Let's say there is a pen on your table. Look at it.

Now take it and hide it behind your back. Look at the table again.

Can you see an absence of pen? All you see is what is there, not what isn't.

Sit quietly, wherever you are, and notice what is real: body, furniture, feelings, thoughts, sensations, surroundings.

Can you find an "I" here?

Or are there just thoughts, feelings, sensations?

If the "I" is linked to the body, how so?

Which part of the body contains the "I"?

If the body loses both legs and both arms, would there be a loss of the "I"?

With your eyes closed, can you find a line between the body and what is outside the body?

Where is "I" located?

Where is the "I" located?

www.LiberationUnleashed.com

If you were asked to find a unicorn,
what would you do?

Would you go on a quest to look for it?

Would you search for it inside?

Maybe look around the room?

How do you know you cannot find a unicorn in real
life?

Stop guessing and look!

Even if your theory is correct, it doesn't help if you don't see it.

When you are hungry and decide to eat, who decides to eat? You or your body? You or your thoughts? Can a "you" be hungry?

Observe when the thought-commentary about actions sets in. Do you first think, "I will turn left"? Or do you turn left and then label this action in your thoughts, "I decided to turn left"? Pick apart all actions and thoughts, moment by moment.

There may be a sense that there's an observer.

You can't shake it, and you assume it indicates an observer.

Well, you can't shake it, because it's a feeling like any other.

You don't have to shake it. You don't have to wrap your mind around it. You just have to see if there's anything behind it.

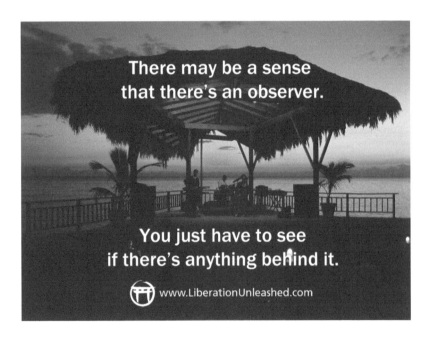

There may be a sense that there's an observer.

You just have to see if there's anything behind it.

www.LiberationUnleashed.com

Are your thoughts possessive in nature?

Do they always have an "I" attached to them? Or are some just thoughts?

An example of this: look at your phone or tablet. Is it your device or just a device? If it is "yours," how did it get to be yours?

Try this on some other things in your life. Are they yours or just things?

Look at a cup or glass on your table.

Is it truer to say that it is "a cup," or a "my cup"?

Where exactly does "a cup" become a "my cup"?

What is the mechanism?

Look at a cup.
Is it truer to say
it is "a cup"
or a "my cup"?

How does
"a cup" become
a "my cup"?

 www.LiberationUnleashed.com

How about the body?

Is that owned, in reality, by a "me"?

As you move around in your ordinary life, check and see if you can find a "self" moving the body around—walking, driving, typing, picking up a cup.

Is there a "who" living your life? Or are there thoughts about everything, including a self apparently living your life?

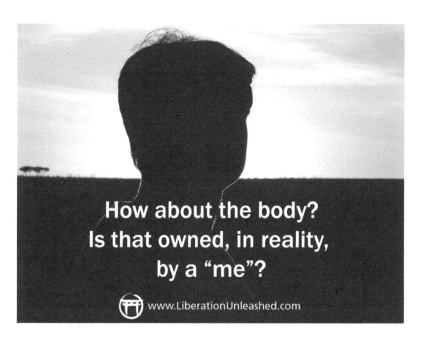

How about the body?
Is that owned, in reality,
by a "me"?

www.LiberationUnleashed.com

If there are no labels and there is just life, what happens to "my" life?

Does life belong to a "me"?

Can you sense, in any way, ownership of life?

Is there a center if it's not labeled "my center"? With closed eyes, find a center. Where is it?

Can you find a line that divides here from there?

If you hear a distant sound, is it heard inside the body or where it happens?

If you were to take a finger and point to "my center" where would the finger end up pointing?

Can you find a line that divides here from there?

www.LiberationUnleashed.com

Imagine having a very pleasant time. Then notice that this is obviously imagination.

www.LiberationUnleashed.com

Imagine sitting on the white sand of a beautiful Caribbean Island, sipping delicious drinks, and having a very pleasant time.

Then notice that this is obviously imagination—day-dreaming.

Now look at the "I" thought, and feel it, and see that it comes exactly from the same place as that beautiful island—imagination and day dreaming.

There is no real entity called "I."

Can you change your thoughts?

Can you say, "I don't like this thought, I think I'll change it" and the first thought gets sent to the trash, never to bother you again?

Or do thoughts simply show up, not controlled by a "you"?

Can you choose your thoughts?

Nothing is separate. Everything is joined. Life flows.

Thoughts, emotions, and sensations come and go like clouds in the sky.

None of them are to be taken seriously. Everything is happening at once without control or obstacles.

Things just flow, light and free.

How about not fabricating anything for a moment,
and simply looking at what's present right now?

Do "you" exist at all?

The Gateless Gate is a concept that points to an event or non-event that radically changes the relation to reality.

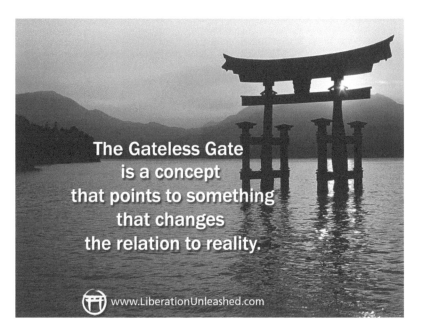

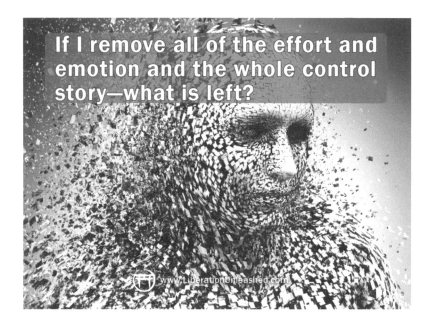

If I remove all of the effort and emotion and the whole control story—what is left?

You can ask yourself, "Now that I know that control was a myth, now that I know that any sense of control was illusion, now that I know that I didn't really have control, if I stop the pretense and remove all of the effort and emotion and the whole control story

—if all of that goes, what is left?

If you can find a park, sit there for a bit, and watch how everything moves and wiggles, how the wind blows, how the clouds move.

If you can't find a park, a view through a window is fine too.

People and animals move. Everything is one movement, including your body, breath, and thoughts.

Watch the totality, and notice—there is no "noticer" separate from the noticing.

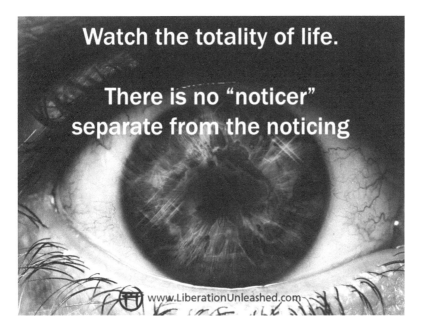

Watch the totality of life.

There is no "noticer" separate from the noticing

www.LiberationUnleashed.com

The "I" is truly only a thought.

It is an illusion. A superb illusion.

This "I" can be searched for but never found in the real world. This truth has been there all the time, right out in the open.

When seeing happens, clarity begins.

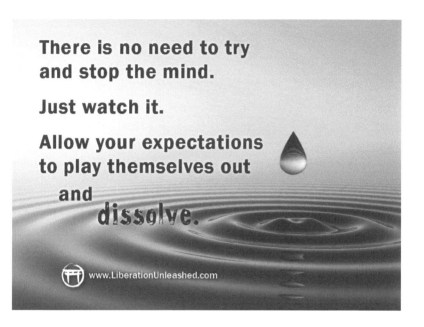

There is no need to try and stop the mind from waiting for a pop.

Just watch it with a playful curiosity.

Allow your expectations to play themselves out and dissolve.

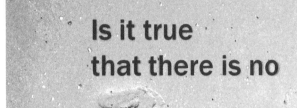

Is it true
that there is no

separate entity,
no "me,"
in real life?

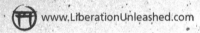 www.LiberationUnleashed.com

Is it true that there is no separate entity, no "me,"
in real life?

The gate is not a personality shift.

It is a perception shift.

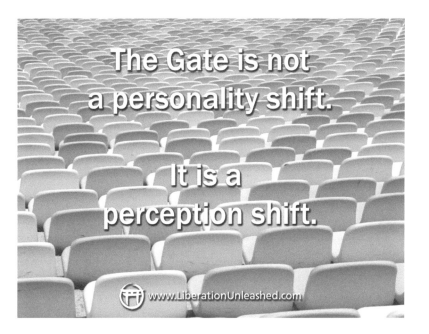

It's very freeing to see how roles play out naturally, and the story unfolds effortlessly.

All is happening to no one, for no reason. Life is simply going on.

It's safe to retire from being the "general manager" of life.

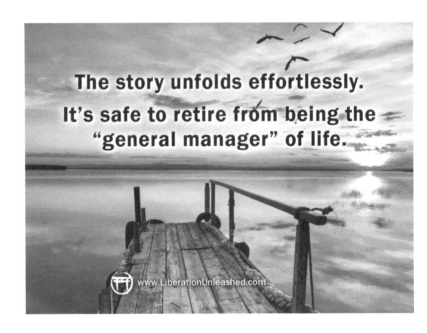

The story unfolds effortlessly.
It's safe to retire from being the "general manager" of life.

www.LiberationUnleashed.com

There is a Zen saying that the birds have no desire to be reflected in the lake, the lake has no desire to reflect the birds, but it still happens.

The birds are reflected, the lake reflects, although the desire exists neither on the part of the birds nor on the part of the lake.

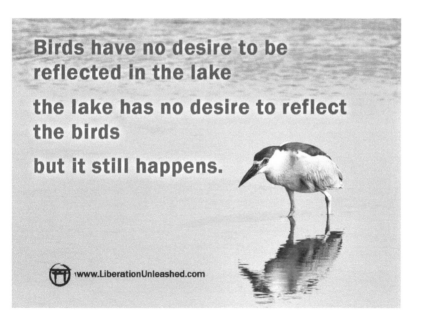

After awakening, identification with self sometimes happens, but usually not for long.

Consciousness unmasks the belief, or life does.

Identification with a story is also part of the story.

Attachment to pleasure and fear of pain are also stories.

There is nothing that attaches. There is only a story about attachment.

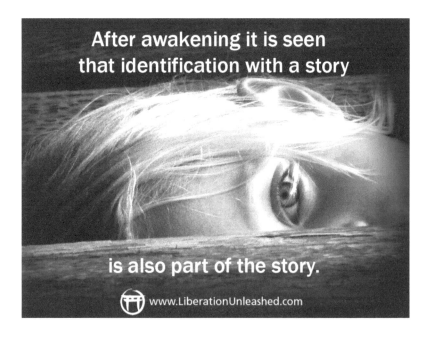

After awakening it is seen that identification with a story

is also part of the story.

www.LiberationUnleashed.com

Does the "I" pop up?

So what!

There is emptiness behind the "I".

Go back and stare at it.

www.LiberationUnleashed.com

There is emptiness behind it. Go back to that emptiness and stare at it. Get familiar with it, focus on it, and let it wash over all that is still arising as doubt. See that the "I" is empty and it's okay for it to be here. It's just a word.

You have to use the word "I," as without it, it would be difficult to communicate. It does not mean that an entity pops up. "I" is just another thought passing by.

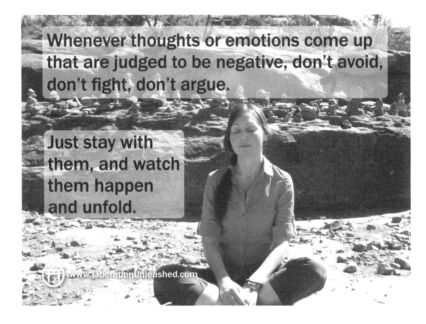

Whenever thoughts or emotions come up that are judged to be negative, don't avoid, don't fight, don't argue.

Just stay with them, and watch them happen and unfold. It's not personal, so it has nowhere to stick to.

This kind of cleanup is obviously not a pleasant process, but you'll likely realize that it actually works.

All you have to do is take your hands off the steering wheel and let things burn when they are set on fire.

What is seen cannot be unseen.

But that does not mean that you can never get lost in the story again.

It's like watching a movie and getting sucked into it. Once you look, you know: it's a movie, not real life.

So once you look, you know it's a story and not reality.

If "you" do not exist, how is there a "you" that is still attached to the body and mind?

There are feelings, there are thoughts, but they just are.

There has never been a self, and these feelings and thoughts have always been here.

Just because you know the truth that you do not exist, and there is no owner of thoughts and feelings, it does not mean they will magically go away.

However, now that the brain has seen through the illusion, why would the illusion of ownership and doer-ship be believed any longer?

There has never been a self.

www.LiberationUnleashed.com

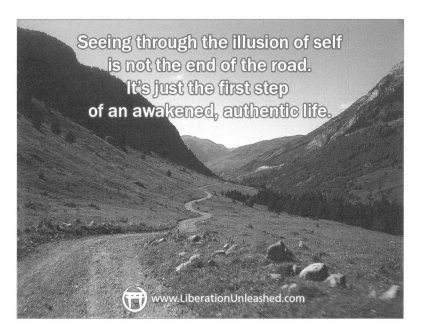

Seeing through the illusion of self is not the end of the road. It's just the first step of an awakened, authentic life.

www.LiberationUnleashed.com

The most important thing is that this is not the end of the road.

It's the first step of an awakened, authentic life.

While the belief in a separate and real "you" may be gone, chances are, a big part of the ego-based structure built on top of that belief is still in place.

How big, only you can know.

It is likely that at some point doubts will come up, reactions that may be considered "not useful" will happen, and (possibly deep) negativity will arise.

The important thing here is that all these things used to cling to, and be fueled through, the idea of self, which is now seen as an illusion.

Please come and join our forum at
www.LiberationUnleashed.com

 www.LiberationUnleashed.com

Acknowledgements

First of all, we would like to thank each and every one of the beautiful people at Liberation Unleashed. You are all truly amazing.

Special thanks and appreciation to Ilona Ciunaite and Elena Nezhinsky, you are the ones that made it happen. Our thanks and gratitude to Nona Parry for helping with the editing and proofreading. Vince Schubert, Solivros Oliveira, Sacha Defesche, Lisa Brooks, Steve Diamond, Sonali Jaidka Kanaujia, Delma McConnell, Laurent E. Levy, Shane Wilson, Jorge Moncayo, Lex Lissauer, Alexey Manukhov, John Christopher, Kelly Sammy, Werner Weissenfels, Derek Cameron, and Elizabeth Whatsleft—thank you for doing all the thousand things that are done behind the scenes: maintaining the LU facebook page and the forum, working on the website quotes app, creating the templates, selecting the cards, and so on.

Lastly, a big thank you to all the people who came to the Liberation Unleashed forum to dance with us for awhile, and to the readers of this book.

This book is because of you.

About Liberation Unleashed

Liberation Unleashed is a global internet-based community. Everyone is welcome to join. It is an ever-growing movement of volunteer guides, here to point you to no self.

All we do here is point. If you are a long-time seeker, or just curious about this, we invite you to investigate and explore what no self really is. This service is available to everyone, for free. Join the forum and request a guide if and when you are ready to see this for yourself. We use the Direct Pointing method, which consists of a dialogue between a guide and a seeker. This is a process of looking at what IS; no prior knowledge or years of seeking are required. The guide poses very specific questions in order to focus the attention on the experience of the present moment. This triggers what we refer to as 'crossing the Gateless Gate': an instant in which the illusion of a separate self is seen through. A shift in perception happens.

We guide because we are a community that openly and freely shares what we have been given by others that did the same for us. We guide because we believe that questioning assumptions leads to freedom. You only need to bring your honesty and curiosity. We ask nothing from you except your willingness to Look.

For more information, please visit our website/forum at:
www.liberationunleashed.com

Lightning Source UK Ltd.
Milton Keynes UK
UKHW050406110422
401375UK00001B/7